Guts

Kai Szala

Presentation by *BookLeaf Publishing*

Web: www.bookleafpub.com

E-mail: info@bookleafpub.com

ISBN: 978-93-95223-61-4

First edition 2022

For my younger self - I hope I'm making you proud.

Self Titled

If I spilled my guts on the table, dear, what
would you do?
Would you pour down the kerosene and light it
with the sparks from your flint-covered soul and
steel-shrouded mind?
Would you plant them in our lazy little garden,
hoping they'd sprout a venus flytrap or a rose,
something, anything, more useful than me?
Would you eat them and turn into a monster I
could no longer take care of, a monster with
glowing red eyes and a beating red heart?
This is why our kindergarten teachers make sure
we keep our guts to ourselves and hold the
planets in line.

So we don't end up like you.

A Fickle Thing

I will chainsmoke you and your love letters.
Let them consume me as I have consumed you.
Let me leave behind this worthless piece of
too-physical flesh.
And join you in the land of the living.

I am not a religious man but I pray that this is
what Saint Valentine died for on that fateful day.

Buildup

Perhaps if I don't burden you with my thoughts,
you won't burden me with your sympathy.
When I built this dam, I hoped it would hold
against the weight of the world. I hoped the
cracks I filled with marrow would be good and
stay in place.
I know empathy doesn't exist and it never has.
How can I place myself into your perfect, rotted
mind? How can you place yourself into my
unstable, glowing skull?
This letter has gone on too long and I'm afraid if
I stay here, digging, the grave will be deep
enough for the thoughts to crawl their way out.

Solemn Sorry

I'll walk with my heart on my sleeve.
I'll run with my stomach in my feet.
I'll crawl with my liver in my fingertips.
I'll break with my mind in the right place.

I've grown so used to being sorry for myself, I'm
afraid of what will happen if I stop letting
myself apologize.

Naivety

The heat of your hand in mine fits perfectly with
the aching of the sun.
And the record player scratches with finality, but
it won't turn itself over.
The planes fly overhead, an ensemble to our
comedic tragedy of a romance.
And I hope when they find our skeletons curled
up next to each other, they'll realize how far
apart two people can be even when so close
together.

Cardboard

I'll keep all my emotions in tiny cardboard
boxes, high up where the water can't reach them,
high up so the rats don't chew through the sides.
Then, when people ask me about myself, I can
show them the rows and rows of neat, tidy,
cubic, little boxes put on display in the
warehouse that I hold in my skull.

I want to watch that warehouse burn.

Perfection's Doorstep

You're the hangnails under the beds of my
fingers.
You're the pain in my neck after just waking up.
You're the splinters embedded in my wrists.
You're the declawed cats paw scratching at my
door.
We could have been perfect. We could have been
perfect. But your festering ignorance mowed
over every wall I set up. Not the walls I built to
keep myself in, but the ones I built to keep
people like you out.

Old Times

The price of inspiration these days has become far too expensive. We used to be able to find it in coffee shops and thrift stores, barely hidden, lying on the floor under the broken table. Now it seems to be on the top shelf, with a locked box and a price tag enclosing it. Maybe I'll go hunting for scraps of it in bins, scraps that line the forest floors. That is where I'll find the corpse of inspiration.

Needs

I want.
I want to live carelessly, consistently.
I want to live perfectly, painfully, powerfully.
I want to live warmly, without judgement or worry.
I want to live freely, fiercely, forcefully.
I want to live honestly.
I want to live. Honestly.

The World's Game of Chess

I've played this game before.
The one where I think I hate myself. The one where I let the world tear me down and shove me into the dirt. The one where I live stone-faced and icy-hearted. And I hated it. Let's play the game where I am soft and easily impressed and loving and loved and caring and cared for. Let's play a new game, one of our own design, one that doesn't need to be following anyone's rules, it just needs to be.

******

It's 9pm and the dogs are howling.
I'll use my last wish to know why they cry so
long in the shortness of the night.
I never get an answer, no matter how hard I try.
But I'll cry like the dogs when I realize how
much I hate you. We barely knew each other and
your betrayal still feels earth-shattering. I
shouldn't cry for myself. I should cry for the
ones you actually hurt. I don't deserve my salty
tears.

Ramble

The ramblings of a madman become the
desperate semantics of a hopeless romantic.
I know you wouldn't love me. I know it. You've
said it before, you'll say it again.
So maybe I'll move on. Maybe. Find my own
footing and my own religion and my own eyes
to see the neon lights.

Absence Makes the Heart Grow Fonder

I think I need some time alone. Just me and my thoughts. Me and my thoughts and the rain and the bees and the paint on my fingers.
I haven't felt perfectly lonely in a while and I think my mind is starting to hate each and every one of you.

Spring

When will winter end? It's a silly question, I
know. A childish question.
But I do truly want to know. It's kept me inside
with my own thoughts for too long and I need a
warm breeze to sweep them away. I need the
flowers to push through the dirt and lift me far
away from here. I need someone to shovel away
the snow at my mind's front door and let me step
into the fresh, kind air.

God, Save the Children

I was spoonfed the lies of the church of masochistic divas, people pretending they don't salivate at the sound of people's screams. They told me the devil likes boys; I heard them whispering about cigarettes behind my back. Maybe if I pray hard enough God himself will lead me out of this hell we've created for ourselves, the one where children are forced into one of two boxes and if they even think about being happy their heads are cut off.

Simple Rhythms

Justice is blind, vengeance is deaf.
Today's worries are tomorrow's sorrows.
Running along the train tracks can only help for
so long, eventually you'll have to cross them.
Swimming under the pier will lead you to the
moon.
Remember to dot your t's and cross your i's.

Soul

The bitterest part of my soul has been hung up to
dry out on the laundry line.
I'll fold it neatly and place it in the back of a
drawer, waiting for the right time to put it to use.
On that day I will feel like the poet, whose only
lover is the pen
and only home is built of paper.
Or perhaps I will feel like the fool
wasting the night away
living vicariously through the star crossed
enemies.

Media, I Suppose

I am going to put my head through the TV if I have to hear one more person who doesn't care pretend to have learned the skill of empathy. The months will fly by before a single one of these fighters against morality ever gains a sense of what swallowing feelings instead of pills will do to your body.

Inspiration

So I drew my sword from the evening sky,
learning the trials of love and war.
And as I lay back, drinking in the view, the
clouds shattered into a kind, gentle rain.
So I'll dye my hair blond and set off on the road,
learning compassion from the most desperate of
fools.

Analysis

The last lightbulb in the hallway finally burnt out today. I think that's supposed to be a metaphor, but nobody will tell me what it's meant to mean. I tried looking it up but all it gave me was a recommendation for some nearby churches. Strange.

Fin(ish)

My cracked skull leaves the story with a finality.
An order, a new page turned.
The last bead of sweat dripping from the faces of
God.
A dying word left unspoken.